MW00711387

A Father's Perspective

Garrick Lee

To Dr. Tim,
Thank you for the
talks and support!
The best is yet to come!

Garrick Lee

Table Of Contents

Dedication

I have got to say that the inspiration for this book came from figuratively seeing me in a mirror. One day, years ago I was watching a movie that really hit me at my core. As I watched I saw how one of the characters had some of the same experiences that I have had. I felt the hurt and the pain that he did. The choices that he made at times I wanted to make. It was only my up-bringing that has kept me from making the negative choices that would bring my downfall. As I got to the end of the film I was elated at his triumphs and at the same time saddened that he had to go through what he did in the first place. Now I am not a real emotional guy but I found myself in tears as I thought about my own life and my challenges with my children. Being that I am a song writer I thought that I should write a song to express what I was feeling. But before I could leave the theater I hear a voice (no I am not crazy) that said "No, write a book". Having never done so, the thought of it was intimidating so I spent a lot of time ducking, dodging and avoiding even starting this adventure. I often would start and stop, I'd delay and procrastinate but finally I dug in and made myself do what was necessary to get this thing done! This book is dedicated first of all to my Father in heaven who gives all fathers gifts, courage and strength to endure this most important task of stewardship over His children who He loves dearly. It is also to all the earthly fathers who choose to serve Him first and in doing that they are able to hear His voice and instructions on how to care for them. To my own father Garrick Lee Handy Sr. He has truly done all that he could to ensure his place as *"Greatest Father Of The World"*. Pops! I love you for what you have given me and my children through me. You are everything that I was supposed to get from God Himself.

Thanks Dude!

Chapter 1

Here's How It Started

I Remember

I want to start by giving a little bit of my own history so that you can know where I'm coming from and as well know that I am as real as they come. I was born in the city of San Diego California having both my Father (Garrick Sr.) and mother (Norma J). In fact, out of the three children that my parents have I was the only one whose birth my father was actually present to witness (he served in the US. Navy). He had been on deployment at the time of the births of my older sister and younger brother so one might say that the middle child was the chosen one (just kidding). For as long as I can remember my mother has followed the doctrine of The Church Of God In Christ (C.O.G.I.C). I can also remember the Sunday morning that my father made the choice to do the same thing. What was memorable about that day is that it was the first and probably the only time that I recall seeing my father cry. I can also remember crying myself and asking my mother why he was crying because it scared me to see him in this way (don't ask me why! It just did! OK!). It was from that day on my parents chose to raise us according to their beliefs in the one true God and His commands. It was then that my course was set in motion as well. Dad and mom did everything they could to keep us on what they believed was the right road to take for our lives. We went to church every Sunday and even most Sunday nights. There was Sunday school, bible studies and even children's church. When I was 9 years old, my parents enrolled me in a private Christian school. It just so happens that the school was founded by the same church that my family attended. It is needless to say that my life revolved around learning about God and the church that we were involved with. Five days a week attending school there was church. Saturdays, there was going to my mom's rehearsals to prepare for Sunday morning at **church**. It seemed to me that there was no life outside of the church. Although it was a good thing to be surrounded by people of like minds who believed as we do, it became a bubble of isolation for me that I would not see the affects of until later in my life. I am absolutely convinced that it was the church or at the very least the doctrine that I grew up under introduced me to a lifestyle of strict rules. I have often referred to it as "the church of the no's". I would estimate that 85% of the things that we wanted to do when we were kids was met by the word no. To be fair I can really appreciate being raised by parents who follow the standards of God and we were taught to obey His commands. But on the other hand, we were not exposed enough to the other side of the spectrum. We were only allowed to listen to certain types of music, or watch television or movies that were not too violent. Cussing, smoking, and drinking was not even allowed to be around us and if we were in an area where these thing might occur, we were pulled away quickly. I must emphasize that it was great to have the protection from as many of these things as possible. However, we were never really taught why it was so important to live a righteous life. For the most part we were strongly told to stay away from anything else. Unfortunately the isolation that we lived left the door wide open for curiosity to run ramped in our minds. It planted the seeds of "what would happen if". My brother often showed no fear in crossing the line to the other side and satisfying his curiosity. I on the other hand was very fearful of the consequences of doing so. As we grew older, we began to explore the possibilities of what was out there. I leaned heavily toward music and its different genres. But as well, the normal tendencies that occur in pre-teens and teens regarding sex and what it was about began to grow. Knowing that this was not something that could be pursued openly, I began to seek out ways to learn about it covertly. I found out very quickly that I wasn't the only one that wanted to have an experience with something that was meant to be shared by a man and his wife. When I was 11 years old

I was involved for the first time in an encounter that would change my life forever. It did not take long for me to realize that I would be chasing this high for the rest of my life. Ironically the place where this first time experience happened was, you guessed it, at **the church**! It happened with a girl that was younger than I was and I really had no idea of how to or even what to do. All I knew was that something was happening to my body and I liked it. One might say that it was like a drug and I wanted to get high as much as possible! So, even with all the Godly teachings and being in a gospel bubble I still managed to step outside of that **"matrix"** and get into other detrimental areas. Over time, I grew in understanding and wisdom and even grew closer to God but still the hunger remained. I did not have an addiction but I did take different opportunities to feed the hunger through high school and on to college. In fact, after high school I became involved with a girl who would later become the mother of my oldest son. We spent a great deal of time together and almost walked down the aisle together but our differences could not be overcome. I know what you're thinking. How could someone who was raised in a Christian home get some far away from the values that were taught from birth? Well I can tell you this it is not very difficult for the seeds of rebellion to grow when you live under very strict rules. By the way, I am not giving an excuse for my choices I am just saying that a desire to experience other things can be very strong when you are told "no" more often than not. Just as a small reminder just because you try to live as a Christian does not mean that you always live as a Christian. We try to do the right thing but sometimes we fall. So on my way to recovery I made the choice to try and grow up and I left home and moved to Tulsa in 1992. I managed to grow up a little more after moving and made the choice to marry a high school sweetheart not too long after getting settled in the new city. I really had no problem with the married life and I do enjoy being in a monogamist relationship. Within four years a surprise came into our lives. After not even thinking that it would be possible, my youngest son arrived on the scene. I became a father for the second time in 1996. This kid took us by surprise but he also took his place in my heart. So here I am married with a new born baby boy and I get an itch that I go to scratch that doesn't involve my wife. Now I am a father of two sons. I have two lives that I have the responsibility to guide through life and I fall one more time. I only have myself to blame. You see when we make choices that do not live up to the plan that God has for our lives, it is inevitable that we choose poorly. So here I am living with regret, remorse, and a whole lot of hatred for my foolishness and still I hear the call that constantly pulls me back toward God and His path for me. I am also forced to re-evaluate the type of father that I am going to push to be for my boys. They need me to be better than what I am doing right now so as a man who chooses God over man and for their sake daddy needs to get his act together. But as a result of my actions my marriage at this point ends and I have transformed into a weekend dad…. AGAIN! I find myself facing me and my choices one more time! But this time it's different. This time I decide to be more than a driving force in the lives of my boys. More importantly, my baby boy must know that his father loves him more than enough to do what is necessary to keep him from making the mistakes that he has made. So here is where I decide to take steps to follow and take heed to the lessons that have been taught to me since I could remember. Here is where I make a real decision to have a relationship with Christ and not just a religious experience. After all, by now I have had enough religion to last for the next twenty years because of my upbringing. I believe that it was my childhood and teen years that caused as much rebellion as it did. My wakeup call came at a dark time in my life. I knew better and it was way past time for me to realize that my Father (Heavenly Father) is well equipped to teach me how to be a better dad. It was then that I knew that I had to grow closer to the ultimate Father, learn from His words, and activate His teachings.

Chapter 2

Part Of The Problem

Let's Get To It

The words that I write here come from years of experience and as life is on-going my experience continues to grow. It is my hope that I will fill these pages with words that inspire, encourage, and motivate us all to a higher standard and a better place. There are many men out there who don't know how to better their situation. There are also those whose words say that they care but their actions (or lack of actions) say otherwise. They are lost because there are few places for them to go to find others that will be on their side. That lack of knowledge can be deadly. Not only is it harmful to the individual, but also to anyone in their sphere of influence. Many of them are at a point of hopelessness. They are in need of renewed hope. So my intentions are to help prevent slow and painful deaths. And hopefully present some solutions or insight on how to deal with the long road ahead. Keep in mind that there is nothing worse for a man than to feel unaccomplished. Part of this feeling can come from thinking that he has failed his family. More importantly he may feel that he has failed himself. This mind-set is a real hardship for those of us who really do give a darn about the well being of our children, the pain can be paralyzing. It is most important to know that the well being of your children is of the highest priority! A man should always be ready and willing to put their own needs and desires aside so that the children are in a better place because of it. If he is a musician and an opportunity to go on the road presents itself, that make have to wait for the sake of a better family environment. The best case is for the family to stay together. Keep in mind that I am speaking of family as seen from the standard of God. Nothing should stand in the way of getting to the most just outcome for their sake!

That is why I am sitting here today putting my thought on paper. I want to be functional in today's society and I want to help others do the same. As a matter of fact, it is part of my responsibility to build others and push them to a better way of life. It has never been enough to be a good person in His eyes and just hope for the best. To not be proactive in the lives of your family is a grave mistake. "Don't rock the boat" is an ideal that can never be successful. It also proves to be a frustrating experience. My own history has proven that to be the case. There are days even now when I want to hit myself for not saying some of the things that are necessary to help improve a particular situation. I have spent many days boiling in my thoughts after saying to myself "just let it go it's not worth it". On many occasions I would convince myself that it wasn't which has become a constant regret that no one should subject themselves to deal with. A father needs to be an active part of a child's life. Not just active, but a positive influence in their life. Children need to know that dad has got their back no matter what happens. I am not saying support should come when his children are wrong, but upholding the standard. I know that positive thinking comes in as many forms as there are opinions but as for me, there is only one source. Ask me and I'll tell you who. Let me give you an example of what an active father might do for his kids. My father would take us on small getaways when we were kids. I say small but to us as kids, it was a real big thing. There were many times when we'd be sitting at a rehearsal with our mom and all of a sudden dad would show up and say to us " get in the car let's go". He would purposely not tell us where we were going and soon we'd end up at the ball park to watch the game. One of the best parts of going was the "don't tell mom" moments when dad would buy us popcorn or peanuts before dinner. Even to this day, my dad loves baseball and still enjoys watching and going to games. I remember thinking many times that I don't like baseball but it didn't matter because dad got us away from the boring rehearsal! For me it was enough to just be with him and not really pay attention to the game. It was a great time to watch people and how they would interact with others. Dad would also take us fishing even though it wasn't his favorite thing to do (he loves it now that he's retired by the way). As well, during those trips came opportunities for him to teach life lessons. These are just a few examples of how a father can change the world through his children. That's love in action, love making a difference. He took the time and he made sure that those times were in abundance and obviously memorable. One of my favorite things to do with my youngest son is to go out for ice cream. For no special occasion we would just go for it and spend time talking and catching up on things. Unfortunately he doesn't live with me so this gives us space to spend those moments together that are really needed to grow a healthy relationship. One of the fun things about these outings is try to get him to eat a flavor other than vanilla. He's what I would call a "plain Jane" when it comes to ice cream. I haven't been successful yet but

I'm going to keep trying until he gets it right. It will happen! I believe it!

Don't Blame Me

We are living in a time when everything is someone else's fault. No one wants to take the blame for anything. As well, any blame placed is met with anger and hostility. The word "responsibility" has become one that is looked down upon in the minds of many and scriptural references such as Philippians 2:3 are thrown out of the window. Most feel that they are entitled to everything and owe nothing for what they receive. "I have a right to this or that" is the battle cry spoken by a large majority of people. Many say that the reason I'm in this situation is because my dad left me or my mom didn't love me. In fact, more than 24 million children (one out of every three) live in a biological father-absent home as sited by the United States Census Bureau. Even though this has become a fact of American life, it is excuses like this that are used in order to dodge any claim to problems that may be caused. Saying things like this shifts blame to others who may not have anything to do with the problem. This leaves the responsibility in the hands of who ever will take it. Of course that also means that there is not a lot of leadership to follow. It also shrinks the pool of standard bearers in our nation. Sheep will always have the need to be lead and this short fall has created many pits for future generations to fall into. Even though some have used this as an excuse, a fatherless society has become more than a reality. A great number of men have made the choice to be more self-serving than to take care of the children that they bring into the world. Some even father many children with multiple women and have no regard for the consequences that it brings. They are foolish enough to think it as a thing to be proud of. How anyone can come to that conclusion is beyond all reason. Truly, now it is way past time for real men to stand up and present themselves with their good integrity in tact. This leads me to a subject that is always in debate "who should take the lead". Who are the wells of wisdom that will take the mantle of guiding not just their own children, but sometimes those who are not related by their blood ties? Sure there are many mentoring programs that exist across the nation, but who is stepping into those shoes. Part of the responsibility of being a man is that we are to help care for those who may not be able to care for themselves. The amounts of men like that are shrinking greatly as the years go by. Their numbers grow smaller as selfishness in men is on the rise. We need to reverse that process and take our God-given place on the earth. So in order to increase the presence of men of good character, we need to move forward without fear toward the basic commands that were given to us long ago. Dads, that means we must be proactive and not just reactive in our family connections. You must have vision beyond the short-sightedness of living in the right now. Wisdom and patience are needed in large amounts in order to achieve at least part of these goals.

He Set The Standard

From the beginning of time there was a standard of leadership set in place for man. "Passivity is perpetuated by the absence of fathers. "Authority is housed in masculinity." This is a quote from a pastor friend of mine that makes as much sense now as it did in the beginning. God Himself created man as the one responsible for rule and command on the earth (Gen. 1:26). He also laid the foundation for the structure of the family. Don't get it wrong I said over the earth not over each other. So don't go telling people that I said that a man should be the supreme ruler over the house (you might get beat up for that anyway)! Besides, the one who controls all the power also has all the responsibility that goes along with it! It wasn't until man, in his own mind-set demanded to be ruled by a king (Refer to 1 Samuel 8:5-8). Man himself rejected God when he became envious of other nations who went against what God has already established. God never intended for man to rule over man. He is supposed to be our king and ruler but man turned his back on the one true king. God knew that men who rule could easily be seduced by a high level of corruption and currently we all can see that His word has come to past. But in his ignorance and arrogance man decided to choose a king. The mistake in that line of thinking is that man is fallible and subject to make decisions that are based on faulty opinions. Being that he is prone to make mistakes, it is easy to see why it was not long before man fell into the hands of the evil one. How can anyone expect consistent stability when a man doesn't even know if he will see the next day? We should also consider the fact that often man is influenced by the emotions of our better halves. You know those that we call wives. We love them with all our hearts but they can influence us to choose poorly based on how they feel at any given moment. I myself have taken many detours based on trying to make her happy or even making her feel better. Food choices have been changed, volume levels of music in the car has been discussed, whether to go out or stay home has been battled over and over again. As you can see it is not difficult to change the mind of a man at any time. He can never be absolutely on point all the time. God will never change His mind therefore it is only God who is all-knowing, and all powerful that is the best choice to lead mankind in every aspect of our lives.

Balance Is The Key

It seems that being a father and a husband can sometimes be a hard road to walk. To say that I am often between a rock and a hard place tends to be an understatement. Here it is that I have four lives that I am responsible for and three of them I don't get to really know them as well as I need to. As is the case with many other fathers, my boys have always lived with their mothers (yes, I said mothers) which causes me to have to choose carefully when making time for them and my wife so that everyone could find their happy place. Is it me or is it something else? I try to keep God first in everything that I do, but it seems that we still can't come together as much as I would like to. Am I thinking too much and not seeking enough? Am I trying to do it all on my own even though I know that is not a realistic expectation? Now you see that is where balance comes into play. It was never meant for us to live a life of too much of one thing and not enough of another. The phrase "do everything in moderation" should have great meaning and is an important consideration in all aspects of our lives. If your body gets too much sun a sunburn is the result, too much of the wrong foods and obesity can occur. Even too much exercise can cause our bodies to be in pain. These are just small examples of how important balance is to us. Our children are gifts from God. When one is given a gift the best thing to do is to treat it with great care and cherish the fact that it were given to you. Time spent is essential of course, but it is not the only thing that is required for balance in our children's lives. Kids need us to not just be in their presence but be active in their lives. If there is a regret that I may have is a lack of activity in the life of my oldest son. I was 23 years old when he was born and my life of course hasn't been the same since. His mother and I were not married at that time and I had every intention of doing what I thought was right by my son. There was only one problem. She and I were not compatible in any way and although my feelings for her were huge, they weren't enough to bridge the gap between us. As a result, we went our separate ways. It was it that point when I decided to move away and change the way I was living. This change included moving to another state. I didn't really consider how big of an impact my decision would have on my son. Even now, two decades later I am still paying the high cost of my decision to leave. He needed me and I was not there to fight with all my might to stay in his life and influence the direction he should go. I'm sure his life would have taken different directions if I had. He has been more exposed to a lifestyle that his mother prefers than one that I lean toward. And my lack of influence may have caused him to not always make the best decisions for his life. I am convinced that he has made choices based on thoughts that do not always set the best examples. Dads, The word father is not just a noun, it is a verb! Your influence is greater than the effects of the atomic bombs that were dropped on Japan in World War II. Take action in the lives of your gifts. You would be surprised at how a trip to the ice cream store goes a very long way. See them as the gifts that they are. Treat them with the care that you would your cars, your televisions, your prized collections, and yes even your precious sporting events. By the way, they are even more important than our jobs even while we need them to support our kids. Don't be the dad that runs the risk of losing those that you support working a job that you may not. They are more than priceless and never replaceable. Besides, the time that we have them is a drop in the bucket of time. Their birth to the time that they leave home is so short and we don't realize it simply because we spend all our time trying to make sure that all is well in their lives. It goes so fast that if you blink, it seems that you will miss some important event in their lives. They get here, we raise them in a Godly manner, and they leave us. There is no way to stop this process nor should we even try to do so. But what if we were able to stop the process, would it really help or hinder them? Think about the impact that would have on them. Who would be satisfied with a life that has progressed to a certain point and just stops right at that point and goes no further? It is our job help push them in the direction of their purpose and destiny. That is the way it was designed long before the word family was introduced.

Chapter 3

What Are We Thinking

One Sided

I want to talk to you all about a disturbing fact. It is a well known fact that the so-called system is quite bias when it comes to the treatment of parents. There have been many stories that prove this time and time again. It makes no sense that even when a father quickly corrects a mistake that is not even his fault, he still can face time in prison. I point out a story from a Houston, TX news station which was posted January 3, 2014. In this case there is no way that the decision made by the court serves to be the best thing for the wellbeing of the child. The child could lose connection with his father and a downward spiral could be created as a result of the judge's decision. As well, the child support that is at the forefront of the case will be lost because the father is in prison. This does not in any way help the child. There are law firms that now exist specifically to service fathers who are trying to get fair and just treatment when it come to custody, support and even visitation for their children. It is not already bad enough that the pain parents cause children when they split up. Our family court system is so one-sided toward the mother that fathers tend to face an uphill battle the majority of the process. Unless he has the financial ability to fight it out in court. Not to mention the hypocritical aspect where support for the child tends to be based on income (Source: www.okdhs.org). I say this because I have experienced no change in my support even though my son's mother has a greater income than I. This is significant because the original calculations were decided by these factors and were never changed when each circumstance changed. We have become a society that praises the single mother and we encourage her to stay strong as she faces adversity. Whereas we need to be more willing to encourage and promote the unity of marriage and I am not referring to marriage just for the sake of being in a relationship. That's great for the moral of strong women everywhere, but a knife in the back of the restoration of the family. Let's not forget that it is the family that is the foundation for great societies throughout the past several centuries. Be it her baby's daddy, working two jobs, or challenging children. All these things show how she is capable of overcoming a great many obstacles. This is all good and please don't get me wrong but, we have in almost every way weakened the authority and position of the father. Here's a case in point (source from news report Jan. 2015). The child can be proven not to belong to a man and just named by the mother as the father (even though that is not true) and he will be held responsible for child support. In regards to the family, we have made him as effective as a broken oar is to a boat on a lake. You see, it is hard for a man to be the head when she is used to being in that position (which really is out of position). It is not possible for him to be an overseer when she is used to being in charge and has no desire to submit to any authority including his. We all know that no house can stand with two masters. That is nothing but division which soon results in a house of cards. A classic example is when I became involved with a woman who already had children we became serious in our relationship to the point of contemplating marriage. At times we would experience different situations that required me to be somewhat forceful with the children, but that was often a fine line when it came to how far I was able to take any disciplinary action. It would especially be a problem when there was a disagreement in our methods. You have to remember that when it comes to a mother and her babies, nothing stands in the way of her protection of them. The problem is that it leaves no room for any other opinion. To her, she is the only one who knows what is best. We have made it ok and acceptable for the woman to be out of place. Keep in mind that I am clear that it is not always her fault that she has been forced into that position. Understand what I am saying, this is not some chauvinistic point-of-view. It is not me stating that the woman should be in the home or bare foot and pregnant, nor am I saying that a man should be beating on his chest shouting about his authority. On the contrary, I believe that all of us are capable of achieving excellence in all that we do. I'm just saying that a woman was never meant to take on the responsibility of headship. Yes she is very capable of leading, and yes she can do the job but it is the man who is supposed to be in that place. Women for many years have had to do what they feel to be necessary to take care of their families. Granted it has also been the man who has led the way in prison population and killing other men and both of these factors have contributed in pushing the woman into that position. Also it is well known that there are many men that are lazy, self-serving, and just good for nothing. Some even take pride in that very behavior. They'd rather waste their time on unimportant things. Who really cares how much money he has or how many cars he has driven? That doesn't make a difference in the bigger picture. It is sad to say that they put themselves in a place where people consider them to be a waste of air. There are also men that have decided that they would go to prison instead of taking care of their children. It's no wonder she has had to take on the burden of head-of-the-house. She feels that she has no choice because a mother hen has to take care of her chicks. It is also a major factor why the fathers who really do try hard are buried in the rubble and are spending a lot of hours having to dig their way out of the craters that have been created by the destruction. I have spent many years with a shovel in my hand with two different mothers in two different states. It presents a major problem for fathers like me who have been put in the same box as bad fathers by the system. Just as all people and men and women are different, so are all fathers.

Is It Really Best

The family has always had a structure and at the top of that structure should be a male leader. Our society has taken him out of his rightful place and in some ways made him inept. Over the past thirty years there has been a slow progression toward that end. But what ever the reason, we still should not govern our country based on an un-balanced system that caters mostly to the needs of the woman and hiding that in the guise of "what's in the best interest of the child". I understand that in years past, women were considered to be the weaker sex and that our governments (state or federal) wanted to make sure that she was treated fairly, but the best way for the child is to have both parents active in their life. A divorce may separate the parents, but it should never separate the parents from the children. We tend to spend too much time and effort in fighting over our opinion of what's best and forgetting that we need to include our children in the process. Yes, I agree that children don't always have a good idea of what's best for them and they will never be given the opportunity to rule my household, but I would say that they know what they are feeling at that time. We would do well to consider how they feel about particular situations. Even though it is true that like most people's opinions feelings can change with the wind but they should not be totally discounted. It may be that there are things the children may be afraid to discuss or circumstances may not permit them to do so. Many times my son has wanted to express how he feels and has not because he was concerned that I may react in a way that would cause me to be upset. In any case, courts should not so easily just hand over power to the mother with regards to children although in every case that I have experienced the burden of proof lies in the hands of the male. He tends to be what I call "guilty until proven guilty". I am very hard pressed not to believe that I would have to spend an enormous amount of money on an attorney in order to get a possible fair shake in a court room. To that end I have a question. Why is it that the male has to prove himself and the female doesn't? Even if she does, the system still leans toward the mother except for in extreme cases. I have found that extreme means that there has to be highly visible signs of abuse before action is taken. The mother would have to be witnessed using drugs or exhibiting some sort of irregular behavior like running after her kids screaming and welding a knife in order to be looked at differently. My oldest son's mother was witnessed on many occasions to exhibit behavior that was quite out of order and that did not change the fact that the state of California would continue to allow my son to remain in her custody. In my opinion she would almost have to be at the point of insanity. It should not be that a highly publicized scene is made before a child is removed from a home. Why does it seem to reason that the children would have to be on the verge of death before they are taken out of the hands of the mother? Why would they have to deal with the possibility of undergoing a lifetime of therapy before change happens? Is this really in the best interest of the children? Now, if that is not a broken system I don't know what is. I suppose that we are to believe that it is in the best interest of the children for them to be at the point of going over the edge before action is taken. I would present to you another possibility. There are thousands of cases where it is just as important for a father to be a major influence in the lives of the children. Yes, it can be a fight but it is also worth every hit taken. Dads need to be pillars rooted with deep foundations in the right sources of information. One of the reasons that our country is in crisis now is that generations are growing up without a strong standard-barring male influence. You can say what you will but there is no substitute for it. Yes, the blame can be placed on the male and female alike but that is not where we should focus. Our focus should be why there is so much blame to go around.

Wrong Thinking

Why this abandonment? Why do males leave their children? Why do they break away from the family structure? What is the draw that makes them abandon their responsibility? I want to look at this for a moment. I believe that there are two chief reasons, disobedience and arrogance. Man has gone so far left that he thinks that he is right. It is fact that no one is always right. It is sad to say that we have allowed our opinions to dominate our way of living. And we know what they say about opinions. "They are like a mouth; everybody has one" (they actually mention another part of the anatomy but this is a clean book so I won't mention it here). But with so many opinions available, how can there be any order in any man's life. If the truth be told, there is only one truth that has any real meaning. We tend to not listen to, or ignore it and there are some that refuse to acknowledge its very existence. You would think that we would learn a lesson from history. When too many voices are given the opportunity to be heard, there can only be one result and that is the chaos that happens when too many cooks are stirring the pot. As an example from recent history, many people expressed their opinion about an incident that they didn't agree with and as a result, riots broke out for several weeks. Even now there are people taking steps to make changes based on opinion that may be flawed. The one voice in this case that should have been heard (that being reason) was thrown under a bus. One can also say that men leave for fear of failure. Men do not like to fail and being called a "sorry daddy" does not make a man feel accomplished. I mean really, what man likes to fail? There's a lot of responsibility in being the head and large amounts of weight that goes along with it. I can say for myself that I have backed out of many different situations because I did not want to face the possibility of failure. What happens if he loses his job? What if he does something that gets a family member hurt? What if he feels that he's not good enough? The list can go on and on. There are multiple reasons and things that a man can face and see as failure. Yes, it can be argued that a man should be strong. That he should stay and fight. But strength alone is not the only thing that is the contributing factor to winning the task. Well, I have seen very few if any men in history that were able to stand alone. There are no corporations that consist of only one man! But because he is supposed to be able to handle it, he will tend to try to handle it alone. No one can build a successful anything by themselves. The outcome is not often good thus failure is a great possibility. Given this scenario, his fear can be so great that he will leave in order not to face it. Another reason is pride and I am not referring to the types that result in positive outcomes. I am talking about the kind that makes us think that we are better than we really are. We are so into "having it our way" that anything else is unacceptable. We've even been manipulated into thinking that we can control the outcome of the fate of the earth. How in the world can anyone think that they can control something that they cannot possible be able to create. We forget the fact that we are fallible and that mistakes are common in humans. True, no one is perfect but there is such a thing as reaching for higher goals and standards. Unfortunately, since we think we are right no one can tell us different. It is a flawed line of thinking at best. It is also a contradiction because no one is perfect. We have to fall on our face before we realize that we were wrong and by then most of the time it is too late. It's very ironic that one major component in man can also cause him to get into a lot of trouble. Although pride can be a good thing, we tend to use it in the wrong way. I take great pride in the fact my sons have a good shot at making great contributions to their generation. But on the flip side, it would be tragic if I was too proud to give them the advice that they needed the most at crucial times in their lives. The only way to correct the issue of the misuse of pride is to seek out a source much wiser and smarter than ourselves. In doing so it should cause our pride to diminish and we can put our thoughts aside to make room for a greater truth and causes that are bigger than just our own circles. When pride can cause one to think that you are better than you really are, we're asking for trouble. Decisions made tend to be selfish which can lead to an ocean of disappointment, embarrassment and pain (Proverbs 16:18). Remember that when we are prideful we will not think of the family first. In that frame of mind it is easy to see why a man would abandon his family.

Is There Anyone Other Than ME

Let's not forget just plain old selfishness. In this day and age, "**ME**" is a very important word. It gives a

sense of empowerment and increases one's self worth.
It puts more focus on the one who means the most to
us. At least it does for that particular individual. Who
would be better to take ownership of it than a man of
this time period? Spending his time doing everything he
can to get what he wants. "Let nothing stand in your
way" can be applied in good and in bad circumstances.
Some of the bad could mean that a person doesn't care
who they step on, hurt or offend to achieve their goal
and God help those who do. Unfortunately more of a
negative conclusion has been the result. We've become
very good at "me and mine". In fact, we have gotten so
good that we would rather lose our wife, our children,
our very family in order to chase that illusive point of
satisfaction. In this case when I speak of satisfaction, I
mean there is never a point where we have enough
money or cars or things. Even though we know that it is
useless to us when we die, selfishness keeps us reaching
for more and more. It keeps us in a loop of " me, mine,
more". With just these two issues alone one can see
how a system of government would opt for the mother

rather than the father. The fact that there are good fathers that exist is overshadowed by those who champion this horrible behavior. It is very easy for children services advocates to choose the party who has had a better history (at least in current history) of being more responsible. Not to mention that women have always been assigned with the majority of the task of raising the children while men go off to fight wars and make the money to pay the bills. I know from my own experience that in a two parent home; most of a child's time is spent with mom and not dad. After all, it is she who takes them to school, afterschool activities and is usually there first when the kids come home. This was very common in situations where dad is the bread winner. Even if both parents are working, mom tends to be the one who assumes most of the duties associated with different children's activities. Things have changed somewhat now, but it is still rare to find an abundance of "Mr. Mom" in our society. In my opinion frankly dad often lacks the patience required to deal with what can sometimes be considered mundane and routine to mom. So, given this "up hill climb" or all the strikes against a man, how is he supposed to find an advantage when the deck is so highly stacked against his progress? In this guilty till proven innocent society it is very difficult for a man to rightfully take his place as a leader of his family. Often he can also run the risk of his family being taken from him when he has the nerve to take his rightful place. It has become a very fine line between a man speaking with authority and being accused of verbal abuse and if he is of any size that just makes it worse for him. Assertiveness is mistaken for being mean. If he chooses to hit a punching bag instead of people, it can be presumed that he may have a history of physical abuse. Insensitivity can be assumed if he doesn't say those three famous words often enough. A married man can even be accused of rape if his wife decides that she is mad at him and tells authorities that she was touched inappropriately (I didn't even know that there was such a thing in marriage). So much pressure can drive a man crazy and to the point of wanting to just give up on everything. A man can find it hard to know if he's coming or going. It certainly doesn't make it easy to navigate through such rough seas. He might as well be sailing on a ship without a rudder, a ship that is also taking on water. I remember being bald up in a corner myself wondering what to do about decisions I had to make that would affect more than just me even to the point of tears. And at the time I was the only one who could be there to help me. So how does he pull off one of the most difficult feats in the history of man? How does he step into his big boy shoes and pants? How does he really become what he was born to be?

Chapter 4

Maybe What We Need

A Leader!

A leader has been described as one who guides or directs. One who takes commands or is in control of a situation. Leaders come in many forms from the captain of a sports team, to the commanding officer of an army brigade; they serve and take others to a higher level or standard. Whether on the field of play or the battlefield, it takes a strong leader to push others past what they tend to believe to be their breaking point. To guide anyone or anything implies that there should be some plan or strategy in place. It also means that there is a means to implement said plan or strategy.

Now, I am by no means an expert, but it seems that it is a position that carries a lot of responsibility and as well a lot of the blame if things don't go well. I've learned in my limited time here on earth that one of the differences between male and female is that males typically are task oriented. That means that their lives continue to move around one job after another. Another way to say it is that a typical male plans a large portion of his life. When he finishes one job he will go to the next one. They see the world as things to conquer. They also tend to tie their self-esteem to the completion of tasks. Having this knowledge, it is easy to see why males are often chosen as leaders (that is not to say that women cannot be chosen as well). Since most tasks require a plan, it is no secret that a man is well equipped to handle the responsibilities of leadership. Please don't miss understand, I am not saying that a female cannot be a good leader. I am saying that from the beginning, the male was instilled with the mantle of leadership. He was born with the much needed tools to be a leader. By the way, it is taught and learned **not a given.** So just because he was born with the tools, it doesn't mean that he knows how to use them nor does it mean that those tools are clean, sharp and ready to use.

He must learn how to do so. This is where my next point comes into play. So what role does a father play in all this? The original design of the family structure or order is that he is first in line with regards to the direction of the family. He carries the weight of all who fall under his umbrella of care. With that weight he is first to make the decisions (good or bad), choices, and to fulfill the visions that will guide the family at present and into the future. His family is priority one! One of the qualities of a leader is to be a visionary. With that being said we must realize they must be ready to act on the principals and guides presented to them by the one who is their leader. A visionary must take the time to study the past to help him see into the future. He should also be careful not to share his thoughts with those who can never understand the approach that he is taking. He must have faith in a source that has more wisdom and understanding than he does and it doesn't matter what his beliefs, he must be ready to receive the directions that are given to him. In my opinion, there is only one trusted source that is the best **Lead** for **Leaders**. That being said, I would tell you that as a leader I am not without many who have shared their life experiences with me. It is the one true God who is the greatest of leaders, but He uses people to pass on his attributes to each generation. One of my examples is my own father. As an adult I have had many conversations with him that have given me the push that I needed to go on to the next level. My dad is not a man of many words but when he does speak, he has many profound things to say. One conversation that I specifically remember is the one that started with the question **"Do you believe that you have been a good father?"** His answer was **"no not really".** Here's why he felt the way he did. For the first twenty years of my life, my dad served in the United States Navy. Fortunately for us, we did not have to move around from city to city as a lot of military families do because most of his duty stations were either a base in San Diego or a ship ported in that same city. As a result of his duty, a great deal of his time was spent away from his family. In fact, with me and my two siblings, mine was the only birth that he was in town to witness. A six month deployment meant that he would possibly miss a first step, first teeth or words, or celebrations on holidays during the year. It meant that he would miss the first rides on bicycles without training wheels. In other words, he missed major moments in our lives. Many can see how he could come to the conclusion that he did with regards to fatherhood. Sure there were times that we missed him and we would have liked for him to be with us. When we were very young it was hard sometimes to understand his absence but, as I shared with him in that same conversation, it was more about the moments that he was able to spend with us that were the most important. Those times were much easier to hold on to and keep in our memories. Real leaders (which are what good fathers are supposed to be) take full advantage of every moment they can to teach good character, strong moral standards and respect for the highest authority and my dad is great at doing those things. When my father was away from us we would take full advantage of the opportunity to play. Now let me tell you what I mean by play. Because my father was the disciplinary, when he was away we would get away with more things since we weren't as afraid of her in that area. It was sometimes a bit overwhelming for her but don't get me wrong because she could hold her own with us. The phrase "wait till your father gets home" had a different meaning for us. Eventually dad would come home and play time would come to an end which meant that the great day of pain was coming for us. This also was the day that my mom's words would come to fruition. What am I talking about? I'm glad that you asked! One thing that I still share with others to this day is the routine that my father had after returning from most of his deployments. It was a bitter-sweet time for us, although we were glad to see that he was home, we also knew that the "when your father gets back" build up was coming close to being paid. Now here is where that routine comes into the picture. Once he returned home, my father would always do one of two things first. Depending on the "build up", he would take care of my mom (The married thing. You get the picture) and then he would take care of the kids. Meaning US! Oh the pain! That wasn't a happy time at all! By the way, dad was real good at his job and showed no favoritism. If we did the deed, we paid the price. You see, one thing that this current generation is not as familiar with is the power and influence of good discipline. Most don't even think that they should have to pay any price at all. In fact it has almost become criminal to discipline a child in public. Parents can run the risk of getting arrested for an act of what should be considered normal discipline. Public spanking can bring the meanest of looks that people can give. Most of our kids believe that they should get respect without first earning it. And don't even think about putting your hands on them. They also believe that they should get respect just because they are breathing. As if they were owed respect from birth. Being able to accept discipline is part of earning the respect that they crave. I find it very difficult to respect anyone who cannot accept constructive criticism. This is just one of the foundational principals that my father provided for us. I have great respect for my dad for helping us to understand the power of earning our place in life because we know that nothing worth having comes for free. He also helped us develop the mindset of consequences. This means that every action good or bad has a reaction. The value of this mindset is that it helped us develop a strong sense of right and wrong. This is also part of what I teach my own son today. He knows that there is a consequence for everything that he does good or bad. I have continued to drill that point home with him time and time again. Do you see how that works? It goes from father to son to grandson and hopefully on to the generations that follow. Each generation can play an important role in continuing this teaching. My father spent those moments with us, and it has become a lesson that is continued to be taught to his grandsons. It is my hope that my sons will do the same for their children. I am happy that they do not have any currently though because I don't think that I am ready to be a grandfather just yet. My father's actions are just another example of leadership in action! Now more than ever fathers need to pass on this attribute to their children. We cannot afford to ignore the need to reinforce these efforts. There are a lot of hurting children who are transitioning into hurting adults that need it. It will help us all in the long run by bringing back a sense of responsibility. It will also help bring order back to our broken down society.

No Expert

Just so we are clear, I am by no means claiming to be an expert on being a father. Nor am I giving a list of statistics of research from different studies. Statistics will change anyway depending on the current trend in whatever think tank is most popular. When you get right down to it, even the so-called experts are not really the first and last word on the topic. The truth is that there is no perfect way or path that imperfect man can present simply because he is incapable of doing so. I, like other men can only express my opinion based on what I've been taught and my own experiences in hopes that my life speaks a truth that is beyond me. Hopefully the way I conduct myself will shine that very light of truth. There is however, a standard beyond that of any man's thoughts or opinions. I do my best to follow it on a day to day basis. Although every day brings a chance of success and failure, my efforts all focus on being better than I was the day before. Though it may be difficult, I must push forward for the sake of others after me always keeping in mind that it is never only about me. Men were given precise instructions on how to live, the management of their family, and their importance of their position long ago. History has also shown that in spite of the specific instructions given, man has repeatedly found a way to take a path that is not to his advantage. His choices have put him in a position opposite of where he should be. As he has progressed, there has never been any other standard that has been more consistent than the word of God or the bible (it was written by men, but it was inspired by God). Because it is the **real truth**, it cannot be contradicted by anyone at any point in history. Though many have tried, it only ends up in their failure no matter how opinions are written or re-written. Besides, with so many different opinions in only ends up being a battle of right or wrong for that time period. Keep in mind that experts said that the world was square. As well experts didn't even know that the continent of North America existed at one point in time. No matter how progressive he thinks that he may be, there will never come a time when a man can trump the authority of the all mighty.

Chapter 5

Reaching Out

They Are Everything

Fathers, one thing that I must mention is something that
we must never forget. Our families are absolutely
everything! Family is the cornerstone of a great society.
I to my own regret, have had some hard lessons learned
and have been reminded of this fact. For example there
was a time in my life when music became more
important and I almost lost my marriage because of it.
In our zeal to provide for, protect, love, and keep the
family together. We tend to overlook this one fact. This
is one example of how a goals-oriented mind-set can be
a hindrance. For some, we will define ourselves by our
jobs. For others, it is their abilities and how they use
them. But what happens to us when we lose the job?
Are we still men? Of course we are but the loss often

puts us in a mode that leans toward a feeling of failure. It's a crushing blow when we measure how successful we are by the job that we have or do. Although the feeling is very real, that does not diminish our family's love for us and we tend to not realize it. When the relationships are strong, being there for us is not a hard thing for them. In fact, I sometimes question the strength of my relationship with my son because of different events that I have missed in his life. I sometimes question how he values the time that we have spent together. Did it add value to his life? Did it teach him some valuable lessons that he will recall when he becomes an adult? The time that I spend with him can set the pace for years to come so I wonder if I have given him enough of my time which is also his time. By the way, our idea of protection is not always the same as theirs. We sometimes think that we protect them by a show of strength, when their mind says that it is just your presence. Sure, I believe that it may be necessary to be able to do all in my power to insure the safety of my loved ones, but there have been many times when just showing up served as a safety net for my son. By doing this, it gives him an example of how a man should be there for his family. When he was much younger, he would stick by my side like glue. For a while that bothered me because I was concerned his that clingy behavior would later become a negative issue in his life. Yes, if invited he would play with other kids, but often he would be right next to me. I often wondered why he would stay so close. I don't think it was always fear of other people, I think sometimes it was a matter of feeling safe with me. He knew that daddy would keep him safe and that I would do everything and anything to keep him from harm. I made sure to let him know that was the case. As his covering, that is my job. I don't do it out of obligation to him, but because of my love for my boy. Remember "family is everything"! A man has to often remind himself of that fact because he often gets wrapped up in trying to make things better for him and his loved ones. The boy (**my twin**) and I have had many occasions where we have spent time doing things that have more appeal for him than for me but for him it is worth the sacrifice of what I want. Often times I really didn't mind though. Keep in mind that he is my son and that a lot of his activities were consistent with things that I have taught him or had some influence in his being attracted to them. Good fathers tend to be willing to give up the world for his kids. They also show more love than they are often given credit for. One reason is because our society has made them the bad guy along with the men who actually are bad for their children. As well, the whole world couldn't come between him and them. Fathers all over the world should do all to set this in place for their children and their children's children.

One Size Does Not Fit All

Many times I think about the things that I have experienced as a result of being a part time father. I've gone without food, rent money has been short, I've had to scrap up money for gas so I can get to and from work, and even the power has been cut off (many times). I've seen $400 checks cut down to $150, walked and biked to a job that I didn't like, and have worked two jobs at once on more than one occasion. I have also taken jobs with low pay just so that I could have some income coming into my household. I am very aware that these things have happened to me partly because of mistakes that I've made. I've even followed a path that is not my own. Needless to say that I have had my share of hard times and sacrifices in order to make things work for me and mine. But even though I've gone through all that I have, there's still no excuse for the pressures that I've had to deal with because of a subject that I'd like to revisit for just a little bit.

Earlier I spoke on a small scale about what I've identified as "the system". One of the main reasons why this bureaucracy exist, (or at least one stated reason) is "for the best interest of the child". It doesn't always take into account that every child and situation is not the same. **One size does not fit all.** The states tend to write rules and regulations based on this very philosophy and put all fathers and mothers in the same boxes for each parent. This simply is not and cannot be a true statement simply because no one is exactly alike. Now I realize that some generalization has to happen, but bureaucrats most often over-generalize the regulations that have been put in place to keep our children safe. This safety is often from a skied point of view. So many children miss out because of the fact that they don't exactly fit the mold formed by these state agencies. Even though there are slight variations from state to state, they each have a blanket policy that is based on those that come from the federal government. Let me reiterate that no one group can or even should speak for everyone. We would not be a republic if that were the case. It is just not reasonable to assume that one voice can speak for all. While I would agree that history has shown that mothers have been the parent that is the one to nurture, I am also reminded that man (that includes woman) is always capable of change. So, what am I saying? In the last twenty or more years, both men and women have chosen to change their roles in society. Women across the board have adapted the **"I don't need a man"** attitude. This of course creates a very unstable situation for the children in these homes where this mindset exists. But even though more women choose to be this way, states still consider them to be the so-called more stable parent. Now before you start calling me a sexist let me remind you that we have proven time and time again that women tend to be the more emotional of the sexes. As such they tend to make decisions based on their emotional state of mind which is not always a positive one. I do commend single moms that have managed to raise their children in a positive manner regardless of the constant battles that they face with their emotions. But I also know that they were never equipped to bring the strength and ability to resolve conflicts like a good father can. No matter what you believe, a mother can never be a father. The "I'm the mother and the father" statement is a impossibility. She can read thousands of books but she can never teach a boy how to be a man. It is not possible to teach what you have never or can ever experience. There are certain traits that are exclusive to a male that cannot be reproduced by a female no matter how rough and tough she is. Humans were never designed to be both male and female at the same time. It is my belief that bureaucrats do not often consider this fact. The progressive agenda of today in fact tries to promote the theory of "everyone is the same" (again a human impossibility). Yes, men have deserted the family and they have also done things to be taken away from the family such as criminal activities. But those men should not be the representation of all men. If that were the case, there would be no men in leadership, none with any money, and especially not one with any authority. Fathers who are truly doing their best to be there for their families suffer at the hands of those same bureaucrats that have decided that **"one apple does spoil the bunch".** I myself have never been arrested, or even been in trouble with the law, yet most of my encounters with the states have been negative ones. Yes, I have been angry many times over the years dealing with the constant battle. I can't tell you how many times that I came out scared and bruised. Too many times I have felt that it was me against the mother who was backed by "the system". To me it has seemed like an up-hill battle to say the least. So many times as well I have felt like I've been treated unfairly. But what has keep me hanging in there is the need to know that I have done all that I can do to be a good father. What has driven me is the expectation that someday my children will know for themselves that I did everything that I can to show them a good example of what a father will do for the sake of his children. It is my hope that within their heart they will do their best to be the greatest fathers in the history of fathers! They needed to know that I would fight to the finish for them, that my love for them is greater than anything that I may have to endure so that they will be in a better state than I've ever been.

Bridge The Gap

I said it before, and I'll say it again. Men, we already have a bad reputation when it comes to the family. So much to the point where even if you are bending over backwards to be a good dad, you're still not always seen in a good light by everybody. Not unless you can erase the memories of others. Our image is tarnished, and in order to change it, we need to make some changes in the way we handle our responsibility. The boys of this generation need men in their lives. They need to be men of great integrity, good character and consistency. We need to be men that will not back down from the highest of standards. Fathers, we need to do everything that we can to be a dominating influence in the lives of our children. Too many of our sons see other things that are more attractive that cause them to pull away from the ways that are right such as selling drugs and even gang affiliation. Dads we must make up in our minds to show up! We do that (**again**) with our presence! I cannot reiterate that enough. No one can affect any situation without being a part of it. We need to fight through all adversity to be in their lives. It is to my own regret that I share this with you here in these writings. Although my son who is over 21 now knows who I am, he does not know me as a father. Unfortunately that hasn't been a reality for him. In his time here on earth, he has spent maybe a year to a year and a half with me in compared to the time spent with his mother. I have spent numerous hours going back and forth with the court system in the state of California mostly to my disadvantage. States have the advantage because they have and make all the rules. But like a lot of men, in frustration I quit fighting and went into retreat to try to fight another day. And most times that day never came. It is very difficult to fight a battle from another state. This tactic always resulted in less time spent with my son. It also formed a wedge between us that still exist today and I don't know how to change our relationship except to keep trying to reach out to him. The situation has caused him to lose the benefit of abilities, wisdom, and love because I chose not to fight. I kept making the choice not to **"bridge the gap"**. As a result, to this day, I do not hear from him at all. Even though I try and try again to reach out to him and want to make a connection. I would love to be a part of his life but he will not respond to my outstretched hands or my pleas for contact. I can't express enough the hurt that I sometimes feel because of days that I just want to hear his voice. I am sure that any parent that has experienced the loss of a child can relate to what it is that I am feeling. I know that I've missed some major events in his life and I'm sorry for that, but I also know that if we try, we can have a great relationship from now on if we work at doing so. Fathers! Do not do what I did because the pain is not worth it. There is no good that can come out of it. Not for you or your children. Sure, there are a lot of hurdles to jump. Yes, you're often fighting an up-hill battle, yes more times than not, you are the bad guy. Is it worth the risk of being in that position? In my opinion, yes! Keep in mind that our relationships with family is more important than anything that we can ever buy or have. There is no possession or amount of money that is more important than your family nor can they be replaced by any of those things. But we must think about what is at stake here. We have always had the burden to support our families. Society is dependent on how we influence the next generation. If we are not there, how can we possibly believe that we can help them? Make sure that you are the first line of defense for what is good and right in their lives. Be the father that you were created to be so that they will have a solid foundation.

Oh How They Change

I've been fortunate to be a part of my youngest son's life in spite of the fact that his mother and I divorced when he was still very young. Our relationship has not been without a lot of ups and downs (that is between his mother and me) but overall I am very glad to see the young man that he is becoming. I know that like any kid that has had to deal with growing up in two different households, that in the past he has had questions as to why he had to live that way. Frankly I am extremely grateful that he is a much better kid than others who have had some of the same experiences that he has been through. He really is turning out to be a good kid who is facing his world with strength and courage. I believe that part of his advantage is that he has spent more of his time with more adults than he has with other kids his age. Now I've had some great things happen in my own life, but there is nothing more amazing than seeing the different changes that have occurred in my son's life over the years. He tends to act older than his chronological age. From the first day he arrived, (I still remember that day by the way) until now so many mile-stones have been reached by him that it makes my head spin. The kid just keeps making me realize that he is on the right track for his life. Fathers that have lived in the same houses as their kids get to see the typical changes that happen to their children. It is very different when you do not live with your children. I didn't get a chance to see all of the different changes that occurred in some of the early stages of his life. I wasn't there for his first steps, but I have seen my son treat me as if I were a super hero. I don't even remember seeing his first teeth, but I do know that I helped him get over the hurdle of thumb sucking. The boy that used to sit on his knees in my car when we would go by a train (he loved to watch trains go by) is beginning to transition into manhood. So many memories of growth in his life have overwhelmed me, and others have made me a proud papa! For anyone that knows me they know that one of my greatest loves in my life is an appreciation for music. I have always taken the time to expose my boy to many genres of music. In doing that it also gave him access to lyrics that are not always the best thing for a child to hear. Well, one day we were on our way somewhere and we were listening to a song with the first word being the "D" word. Did I mention that my son has liked to sing for as long as he could talk? He was probably no older than 7 or 8 years old when he began to sing the first word of the song and I laughed to the point of almost having to pull the car over. Of course he didn't really know any better. To him, it was the enjoyment of the music. At that age it was just a word. Needless to say, I had a little talk with him about saying certain words that he shouldn't say. But the fun of just sharing a love for music is one of many moments that we have had together and today he is beginning to write his own music as well as carve his own opinions of what he likes and doesn't like. Over the past years there have been other moments that have been great indicators of change in my boy's life like the day he came over and I noticed that he was starting to grow a mustache. On many occasions he has said things that would come straight from my mouth (dad this should let you know that they are listening to you). It still amazes me how much we think alike. It is also funny to see his confusion when I tell him exactly what he is thinking. This is a sure sign that my influence plays a major role in his life. He would often make different statements at a younger age that he would get from copying me and although it was funny to me, I still had to remind him that he was too young to say what he said. You see, sarcasm runs deep in my family roots and he made a sarcastic statement that clearly would be something that I would say and it was too old for a youngster to think of, but he did. These changes have been happening, and will happen throughout both of our lives, and to see them makes me proud to be his dad. I remember when I first heard both of my boys voices change. I thought to myself is it that time already? Where did the little kid voice go? One knows that it will happen one day, but it was so unexpected. Wow! Where did the time go? My response was "who are you and what did you do with my little boy"? It is inevitable that things like this would happen but they always happen so fast that it seems that there is no time to adjust to them. I sometimes find it hard to believe that I could be part of lives with such potential but I also count it as a privilege. As I think about the minimal time I have spent with both of my boys, they both have managed to take on a lot of me in them. Not to sound arrogant, but I have great hope for them being that my own foundation has been so solid. I have had and still have a great father in my life whose name I carry. The boys have big shoes to fill in carrying on our legacy. Yes, they have their own path but it is legacy none the less.

Chapter 6

Fathers Are Key

You're More Important Than You Know

Remember that I said earlier that men tend to define themselves by the job that they work? While that part is true to an extent that is only part of the whole picture. Like a building needs strong foundations on solid ground, the family needs a father, a husband, a pillar that plays a major part of holding it all together. Too many times men lose sight of this true fact. We don't understand or won't except our importance in God's plan for the human race. So much time is wasted because we are chasing things that are really insignificant but we think that they mean a lot. Men, why are you important? Well I'm glad you asked! You see our job is to be God's representation here on earth.

We are to present His holiness, His truth, His integrity and most of all His love. Dads, do you really know how powerful you are? Do you know that if you are taken out of the puzzle there is always a piece missing and that the picture that is presented is never complete without you? There is always a hole in the picture when you are not there. I myself have never had to go without the support of both of my parents. But my father has done everything in his power to be a great example of God on earth. This is the person that we are to be. We represent truth by making up in our minds that it is worth all the trouble of being straight forward in every circumstance. It is easy to make something up off the top of one's head. It is yet another thing to have to keep up the lie and having to remember what was said before and keep it straight (it also tends to be way too much trouble to do so). We represent integrity by taking our jobs seriously and standing for truth whether or not it is to our advantage. No matter what the job is, we take ownership. I personally work as if I'm being watched all the time (even though I am not). That's because I am. No matter what you believe, there are eyes watching you all the time. They may not be human or physical eyes, but they're watching none the less. Those eyes may be in the back of your mind in the form of a wife and or kids depending on you to come through with provisions for the household. Or maybe time spent helping with homework or even house work. Having good integrity opens the door to one thing that a man treasures a great deal more than most. That thing is "respect". In most cases, a man we'll be ok not being liked. But when he loses respect, it hits him at his core. I don't know about you, but I'll take good integrity any day. Then there's His love. We can't possibly compare to the love of God so I won't even try. But I can say that when we love like we are asked to love, it produces a response that creates those strong pillars that supports the whole family. We can show our love by showing consistent attention to details. In order to do that, planning is the key. Guys we are already built to plan (we are visionaries remember) so we do what we are good at doing. Keep in mind that if we need to turn off the TV than that's what we need to do. Sometimes we may need to adjust our work life for the sake of family time. I have friends that believe that to do so is a no-brainer but to some that is a hard choice but it may be necessary in order to show our love for our loved ones. Financial support is absolutely important but money will never buy time or presence. Guys, never forget who you are designed to be. You are foundation! You are glue! You are strength! No one can replace you when you are firing on all cylinders nor was anything supposed to do so. I'm not taking anything away from mothers, but when the head is thinking and doing things at the top of his game the body has no choice but to follow and will do so willingly.

What Difference Do You Make

When my boy was much younger we would make plans and go on adventures together. These adventures still occur today. We've gone from soccer practices, games and cartoons to soccer practices, games and super hero movies. In between those transitions there have been many trips to the ice cream shop, lots of pizza eating, and plenty of wrestling (with a little tickling in between) matches. We also fit in conversations about life and living with all of its ups and downs as well as his hurts and the things that he likes to do. Very often during time spent, there would be opportunities to share with him and teach him about life and standards that I have set for him and those that he should set for himself. There have even been moments that he has witnessed me in anger and frustration and in those times I have done my best to show him how to work through whatever issues without making a bad situation worse even to the point of shutting my mouth when it is necessary. I believe that part of being a good man is learning how to maintain a sense of control of one's mind and attitude when faced with difficulties in life. Keeping that in mind I'm very sure that my boy hasn't had to see me blow up and go off on anyone or anything. While it is true that in my mind I should always be ready to fight, I've known for many years that actually doing so would set in motion a mindset that will affect my boy for the rest of his life. So even if I wanted to fight physically, I knew that my strength for him comes in being better at fighting with my mind and intellect and that would always serve him better as he lives him life. I have taken a lot of time thinking about, hoping for, and praying that the impact that I've had (and still have) on my son's life has been a strong and lasting one. Good men whether you are a father or not should always consider the effect that you have on those that you may influence in your lives. Children and teens everywhere need to have a firm foundation that is reinforced by the truth. Keep in mind that there is only one real truth and it does not come from man. That means that we have to be guided by much more than our own ways of thinking. Even if you don't believe in a higher power, I cannot emphasize enough how your having good integrity can create major changes in the lives of many. Believe it or not, you mean the world to even those that you may never actually meet directly because of who you have influence over in your circles. Think about it. Many leaders over the centuries have influenced millions of people without ever having direct contact with them. Political and religious leaders do it all the time with the platforms afforded to them especially with the continual rise of the use of social media. You as a leader have the power to create life or cause death and that is a very powerful position. I'm not speaking of literal death of course. I am talking about other people's goals, dreams and aspirations. You have been given the highest responsibility to keep the standard and the order in a world that constantly stirs up chaos. Yeah! That's a tough task with big shoes to fill. But you are equipped to the job that you have been given. Before you were even born your DNA and your soul was packed with all the necessities to take on all the challenges that you would ever face. So you can take courage and be confident that you do make a big difference to those that are important to your journey. Your contributions to your family can and will change the world. The question is will the changes be positive or negative.

This Is Bigger Than You

I recently saw something that I know has changed my outlook on my place in the family. It made me think about what it is that I am doing or not doing to make sure that my family continues to move forward and into greater success. What I saw was a scene that has been played out time and time again in homes all over the world. It is universal no matter what your cultural background or belief. So here's the picture. You have your typical family with its normal back and forth, give and take relationships. The kids get older and the gaps between them and the parents grow larger. Finally an incident occurs between father and son that escalate the situation to the point where the son decides to leave the home in anger. Of course dad is fine with his departure because there can only be one king of the castle and he will not stand for being disrespected. So as time goes on the son begins to come into his own, and build his own life. He later has an accident at work that causes him to be temporarily disabled and unable to walk. He moves back in with his parents and obviously he is depressed and not easy to get along with. As well his view of life is one of "I'm good for nothing" which means that he has no motivation to do anything. Now at the height of his frustration, dad takes matters into his own hands and picks his son up out of a wheelchair and takes him outside. Knowing that his son cannot walk, dad stands his son up and places him on his back and walks with him carry his full weight. This same scenario goes on day in and day out rain or shine for a good amount of time and the whole time dad is encouraging his son and telling him that he can make it. After some time the son begins to again walk without assistance and his relationship with his father is made stronger as a result of time spent and continued strength from dad. What gets to me the most is that the father literally carries his family member to the next level in his life! How many times have you been asked to carry more than your share of the load for the family? How many times have you realized that you have to see the bigger picture? Visionaries (which are what you are) have to see what others do not. Even when others don't agree with you, it is up to you to keep them on track on the road ahead. You set the tone and hold the key to the direction of your family. But because of that, there are more requirements for you to take on. This is bigger than you and at the same time everyone is looking at you to come through and make it right. Strength is needed and it should come from only one source. I believe that it comes from our creator and that He works through our connection with others. We can never do it alone so I would admonish you to connect with like-minded people who tap into the same right source as you do. I'm glad to say that to the best of my abilities I am able to carry most of the load for my family but I also know that I am not alone. Every day I look to get my instructions so that I can live each day to the fullest! Men, don't be the one to think of going solo. There is too much to do and there is too much to take care of for your loved ones. The actions that you take daily can and will influence many. So what steps are you taking to turn your world into an oasis in the desert?

Chapter 7

Don't Force It

Their Dreams Are Different

I have spent a lot of time talking about one child in these writings. I actually have had the pleasure (and the pain) of caring for three children. Unfortunately two of them I've only been allowed part time access but in the time that I have been given, I've discovered that the hopes and dreams of each of them can often differ from those that I may have for them. By the way, that is not a bad thing. It is not uncommon for parents to try and live their lives through their children. Things that they were not able to do or did and may want to change in their lives are sometimes forced upon the children. To those parents I say that you know it's not right, but you just can't help yourself. Just in case you didn't know moms and dads, your dreams only die when you let them and they have nothing to do with your kids. Always be mindful that just because you have a major part in raising your children that doesn't mean that they think like you. My youngest son and I have been able to spend the most time together and I get to see quite a bit of me in him. Even to this day he is amazed at how I am able to tell him what he is thinking and often times I am right on target. Our closeness has allowed me to have many talks and adventures together with him and that in turn keeps me in his head so to speak. I would say that he gets over 75% of his personality from me so that is not too difficult for me to be in that position. I often tell him that I know what you're thinking because I know myself but he is still surprised. But even though we are the same, I am very aware that we are very different. He has goals and dreams that I never even got close to thinking about. I couldn't see myself wanting to be a pilot or an architect (he is still making up his mind) when I was growing up but he does. He also participates in a sport that I never looked into playing. I still don't like the sport as he does, but I've learned to get along with it. He has even had experiences at his age (right now 17) with other races that I only dreamed about. I have yet to go jet skiing on the lake with my friends. Come to think of it, I don't have any friends that go jet skiing at all. I am so jealous! These things have caused us to have different likes, courses and pursuits and that is okay because I was never meant to produce an exact duplicate of me. My wife would say that's a good thing because I can sometimes be a boring person. I very much want his dreams to be different from mine because his destiny can never be the same as mine. In fact, my desire is that it is much greater. Even if he wanted to be exactly like me he couldn't be. Any parent would have an unrealistic expectation to want that for their children. God never intended for anyone to be exactly the same. My boy is truly becoming his own person and I am very glad for that fact. He is beginning to find his own pathway to and through life. The steps that he will be taking are the ones that he will choose and the fears that he may have will have to be swallowed and overcome by him alone. I am now looking at how and when the reins will be transferred from me to him. This is a very exciting time for him and me because we both get to walk through these next life changing steps together. Dads, your man child has no business taking over dreams that you may have for yourself. Even if you have a desire for him to "take over the business one day", that is not your call no matter how much you try to steer him in that direction. Remember that each of us has his own destiny to follow and what is for you may not be for him. That is selfish of you to do that to your child. There is no rule book, or writings that give you that right and don't ever believe that just because you are the man that gives you the right to be the dominating tyrant in the lives of your inner circle. Men, we are used to having control because it helps us get through most situations but this is one thing that will always be out of our control. So you should not go to the trouble of trying to manipulate your way into it. "Their dreams will always be different".

Your Role Is Love

Fathers everywhere struggle with what some of them consider being a four letter word. The word **love** is one who's real meaning tends to escape men in general. We already don't do well with our emotions and love may give us the most trouble. Men have often been taught "don't let them see you cry". Phrases like "suck it up and be a man" or "take it like a man" all imply that we are to be tough. Tough and love often seem to be complete opposites. We're supposed to be able to take the hit, shake it off and move on. But if we don't adhere to these **"man rules"**, we're called sissy, soft or even coward. I remember as a boy growing we would play many games that challenged our toughness and bravery. One of which we dubbed "Smear the queer" or throw-up tackle. It was a spin-off of football where the ball was thrown in the air and who ever caught it would try and run for a touchdown. Your toughness came into play because it was you alone who faced however many players there were playing the game. It was a game that caused one to get bragging rights for the one getting the most touchdowns which is another rule in a man's play book. I remember playing one day and I caught the ball. As soon as I got it I was confronted with a guy that was twice my size. He grabbed at the waist but I was so determined to get to the goal line that I somehow bucked and flipped him over and got loose and ran for a touchdown. I guess it was my **love** for bragging that keep me from being stopped from reaching the goal. By the way, I ran for over 50 yards on that play. I'm just saying. So, what does any of this have to do with "love"? That's just it! None of it is even similar to the meaning of the word. I would even say that it goes in the opposite direction. So when you keep this in mind, it is not hard to come to a conclusion of why men are so deeply rooted in the other side of this highly important emotion that actually can make us better men overall. Men everywhere see love as a gap in his armor of defense. We can't let anyone past a certain point in our mental force field. To do so will show our own vulnerability and that is a no go! Well guys, here's what

I have to say to you to offer as a solution. **"Suck it up"!** And in the words of a famous wise Jedi, "you must unlearn what you have learned". Many things that we learned as boys about men are way out of line with what we know to be the real truth. It could sometimes be like trying to unscramble an egg. We are to use the tool of love to strengthen, encourage, and awaken the dormant areas of the lives of wives and children. Remember, we are to be the heads of our households which means that we are to set the atmosphere in our homes. What better way to set the pace than with love? For example, a wife is at her core a receiver. So what she receives is usually given back in multiples (give her your seed, she gives you a baby). When you give her your genuine love what she gives back seems like an endless array of love in response. She cannot help it because you are feeding her a major component of her emotional diet. Your love keeps her in a place of peace. When she knows that you have her back, front, and sides she has no problem holding up her end of the deal (meaning your marriage). Here's a hint. Figure out what she likes and give it to her! For some women simple words give her what she needs. For others simple items are a key to her happiness. But like all things with the human experience, we have to take the time to find the best fit for your situation. Seems simple enough but it sometimes means that you have to compromise and so what if you do! Again the ultimate goal is to promote love throughout your home. Now let's talk about how it helps the children. From day one of life we owe them our love. It provides the encouragement that they need to accomplish major things in their lives. Think about it, before a baby can even turn over your smile can cause him to be active in so many ways. When he begins to stand, your reaching out to him can cause him to walk. When he falls, the love from mom and dad helps to dry his tears. These things that we may consider small or even take for granted can play a very pivotal role in the development of our children's lives. Dads, how many times has your love for your son made you spend numerous hours teaching him how to be better at his favorite sport or on the road taking your daughter to ballet classes. It is my belief that a son tends to want to be like dad before he even reaches the age of five. I could be wrong, but I'm betting that I'm not. Do you even realize how impactful that is on their lives? When daddy loves them like that they feel that they can do anything. How powerful and comforting is that feeling for them? As well they have no problem giving back the love that they have received from you. What about when the boy gets a bad grade in school? Is it not to his benefit to help him improve in that particular subject? That shows your love and he will not forget it! That becomes a big push to his greatness. What about the first time baby girl's heart is broken? Instead of going out to break someone's neck, who should be there when she needs a shoulder to cry on? Daddy the protector/consoler! That's who! There are so many opportunities to show your love to your kids and I'm sure you would agree that I've only scratched the surface. I can't express enough how important your love is to your kids. You hold the key to propel them to different levels in each step of life. Dads, if you can't tell by now, you showing your love is not a mushy waste of time. Nor does it mean that you are soft or weak. On the contrary, it shows you are very powerful. More than any superhero could ever be. I am absolutely sure that my dad made a lasting impression on me by showing his love for me through his actions over the years. His impression even shows through me to his grandsons and they are very aware of how his influence has shaped their lives. The way that works is earth-shattering how a man can reach past one generation and teach another!

Chapter 8

They're Watching

It's Not A Faucet

Let's face it guys. We can be cocky, too sure of ourselves and just down right over confident. After all we've worked hard for whatever achievement that we have conquered. We scored the winning point in the championship game or closed the deal on the big sale that put the company on the map. We made it through the times when money was tight and good jobs were hard to find. We seem to have a built in sense of how to turn up the intensity when it counts. We have that gut feeling of knowing when to dig deep and continue to push forward in spite of the odds and no matter what we're going to get it done. All this gives us many reasons to be secure in our confidence. While it is true that most of these things are a part of us, we forget that we have to make the choice to tap into them. They are not automatic. No one's "super abilities" kick in just at the right time. We make the decision to step up and do it. But for all the things that we seem to be able to just turn on or off by choice, there are a few things in our DNA that were never meant to be controlled in such a manner. They have to be learned and studied over and over and you never stop growing in these areas if you're smart. In other words they are not a faucet that you can turn on and off and to be good at them we must always keep looking for ways to be better and better every day. Do you want to know what these areas are? **Oh course you do!** They are being a husband and a father. Your life as a husband is ever changing like the direction of the wind. Remember that we humans change our minds all the time. So it is not a reach to see that each day cannot be the same day in and day out. Our wives can be "bone of my bone" or "this woman you gave me" depending on the day and how they feel! Learning how to navigate the waters of marriage is an on-going process with the end of the lesson being death.

At least that is the best case scenario. You can stop being a husband, but you can never really turn it off. I spoke of other things that are innate in us and no experience that we have can change them. But beyond that not long after man was created God Himself decided that it was not good for him to be alone. So from then on the husband switch was turned on with the All Mighty having no intention of turning it off. So, what about being a father? This too is something that we learn and learn and learn. Do you get the point? Isn't funny how our individuality can bring about unlimited possibilities. Each child comes with their own set of circumstances. It again says that for constant change, means constant adjustments. Even though God has set forth a standard for us to follow, each person has to make a choice to stay in step with it. As a father, I have to make decisions that affect my children's lives from that point on. So with human nature ever moving forward, I cannot always be on target with predicting what will happen with them accurately. But who wants to always be right anyway? That's too much pressure!

It is also not humanly possible! Knowing these facts, it is easy to figure out that a father always has to be a father and he can never turn it off. I know, I know. It is easy to be a "baby daddy". You can do the part time thing and when things are going well, you are right there in the mix. But when it gets bad or undesirable, you are gone as fast as your feet can carry you! Talk about cowardice! The dad in this case feeds on convenience. He knows how to set himself up as the good guy with the kids but behind the scenes he does what he can to do as little as possible. The word lazy comes to mind when you think about a man like that. But if he's really good, he can stay the hero. This dude is really good at wearing a disguise. It is deception at its best. At least until the child comes into his own understanding of life. At that point children can see what he is really about. His shine may lose its luster when their eyes are opened. This is where a father's good integrity is a plus for his kids. He can use this attribute to help them integrate better into society and prepare them for facing many obstacles. When a man is determined to live a more structured lifestyle, it is not likely that he will settle for being less than what he can be. Maturity has no choice but to come shining through. He also won't waste time dealing with things that don't really make a difference in the big picture. Have you ever heard the saying "don't sweat the small stuff because all of it is small"? Well that is him all over! With that frame of mind he cannot afford to compromise on some issues and be double minded in others. I'm not saying that we should be 100% all the time because he can't be, but I do know that we should push for more than normal each and every time. Mediocrity should leave a bad taste in a man's mouth and he should want to stay far away from it. I mean as far as the east is from the west. Our families deserve our best efforts and nothing less.

Monkey See Monkey Do

We've all heard the saying, but do we really think about the validity of it and how it affects our children? I came to the conclusion a long time ago that I am a mixture of my mom and dad. Some people are heavy with one or the other, but I can truly say that I have a pretty good balance of each parent. For those who know my parents they are aware that both of them have real differences so I can at any time be pulled in one direction or another. Part of me loves the structure that has been drilled into me by my military father. Most times he seemed highly focused so guess what? I tend to be highly focused. It gives me a sense of direction and a will to complete my purpose in life. That mostly makes it a little easier to achieve the goals that I set for myself. He was the one who taught me to always have a plan, and to have a back-up plan for your plan. That line of thinking allows you to grow your ability to think on your toes. It gives me clarity in otherwise tense situations. Then there's the other half of me that is my mother. She is the fun loving, laugh out loud side of me. The artistic, free thinking aspect that is in me also comes from her. She is a people person and although I am not always good with people, I see myself as one who tries to do the right thing when it comes to others so I guess that kind of qualifies. I'm sure that because of her influence I have become a dreamer. I am able to hold on to things that are bigger than me because of her. It is her pushing the gifts in out when I was much younger and did not even come close to seeing the value in them. I am a "glass half full" type of person and I'm sure that my optimistic attitude also comes from her. She has always told me that "things will all work out" and I hear her voice in my mind in times of trouble. Both of my parents are big givers although most times my father gives because my mom told him to do so. I am convinced that this is why I get into so much trouble with my wife because I give and I give without expectation even sometimes to my detriment. With such a mix of personalities that are so different, it is no wonder people have told me that I am weird. I find it hilarious to see the reactions of people when I say or do something that they don't understand. Their reaction in no way hinders me from being who I am unless it causes them to be hindered in any way. Overall, I'm okay with my personality. I'm sure that I am misunderstood often but that's to be expected when you tend to be a bit unpredictable. Parents that use wisdom look to monitor how they act and react to situations that they face around their children. They are very careful to give an impression that comes from right thinking and the knowledge that they are being watched and they will see the result of their behavior later through their children. Kids tend to want to be like those who influence them the most. Not surprisingly my son has followed that track. This is one reason why I have been very careful throughout his life to be a good example to him. I made a promise to myself early in his life that he would not see me act in a negative manner as much as I could control it. This promise is not always easy to keep. It is especially difficult when I have to confront not only his mother, but her husband as well. Let me tell you that there have been many times when I wanted to put a hole in more than just a wall but I have kept the promise in the back of my mind and have kept my cool for the sake of my son. Hey dads! See how the kids watching us can also keep us from going jail? That is fantastic! I am watching this kid and it is freaking me out to see how much his thinking is similar to my own. I mean, I am very present in his life which means that he watches me and follows my lead, but I still expect for him to develop his own thing, his own way of thinking and doing things. Do not misunderstand, he is his own person but I see me all over him. He has however managed to cross over into different worlds that are somewhat foreign to me which allows him to tap into things that I could not expose him to. I also believe that he has already surpassed me in some areas. I fully have an expectation for him to do exactly that. But the base of his personality comes from his parents because from day one, we were his only influence. It seems that the parents of this current generation don't always adhere to the fact that the way that they live, can become a pathway or even a detour for their children. They don't see how their wreck-less actions lead to wreck- less children. There are many examples of this all over social media that is shown daily. For example, kids setting fire to themselves or cutting off the air supply to their brains. This type of behavior is wreck-less as well as stupid. From the 4 year old that copies his dad acting like a gangster, to the ten year old that loves to cook like mom it is easy to conclude that our children follow our lead. I cannot emphasize enough that parents have the awesome responsibility to show kids the right way to go and to keep showing them the way to go. Also it doesn't just end when they decide to leave your home. It continues until the end as long as we allow our relationships to stay together. As proof, I still do many things the same way my father does and I haven't lived in my parent's home for over twenty years now. I have said many times that my son is like me, well I am so much like my father that people that have not been around both of us at the same time are very much convinced that I am an exact duplicate of Garrick Sr.

Things Are Changing

We are seeing a growing and disturbing trend that is occurring all over the nation. It is mind-blowing to see this because for decades we have seen more stability in this area but now we are slowly seeing a turn around. I believe that it is a plus for some fathers but a blow to the structure of the family. I find it interesting to see it happening because it shows that we all are vulnerable to the detours that can become major distractions for raising our families the right way. What I'm talking about is the fact that we are witnessing more and more females being in trouble with the law. There seems to be more of them that cross the line in that area. Women everywhere are neglecting the family and home. There are a growing number of incidents where it is reported that they are committing acts of violence such as fighting and bullying. As well to add insult to injury, they are showing no remorse for their actions. By the way, that has historically been a male trait. Also on the rise is their usage of guns to commit criminal acts. Women are even using drugs at a higher rate. Single mothers are acting more like their children's friends than their leaders. Kids don't need their parents to be friends with them they need guidance to get them through the obstacles of life. As a parent I can't possibly believe that it is ok to be on the same level as my son. We will always have great playful relationship, but we will never be on the same playing field. I will always be his father. I am not saying any of this to celebrate by no means. No, I'm not happy it at all about this dilemma. On the contrary, it is quite alarming to see such a decline. If our mothers and fathers are both becoming largely self-serving and more apt to having a "do what I want to" attitude, what hope is there for our children to be lead to the right path? It would seem that family service agencies are now being required to revamp some of the current practices and procedures that lean more heavily toward mothers being the better choice for kids to be placed with. I do however believe that this is even more of a reason for dads to return to their roles as leaders of the family. It is a sure sign that what has been the established standard of leadership should be adhered to in a major way. Also the scales that have not been in your favor are beginning to shift to a more balanced situation. Dads, we really need to stay on point with our connections to our kids. The decline of the lifestyles that we are seeing in more and more women give kids nowhere to turn. We need strong fathers who make the daily choice to walk in their authority. Without them we end up in dysfunction. Has anyone else noticed the subtleties of this happening already? It is so much in fact that society sees it as normal. In this politically correct climate people have redefined the definition of family. But their definition only serves the finite minds of man. Man's mind can never fully understand the thoughts of the creator. If he tried it would fry his brain! Man is no match for the Greater One! He would be insane to even try to compare.

Chapter 9

What Do We Do Now?

So! What Am I Saying?

In this country we have made some major changes to the world stage. We have set the standards that others reach for and try to follow. The western world has been a magnet for millions to come be a part of groups of people who do everything they can to carve out their share of the pie. America has truly become a land of opportunity. Many have suffered through hardships and made it through great pain just to get into this country. We have grown into a major power in the world that we live in. I am reminded that we were founded on beliefs that a higher power guides and leads us every step of the way. It has been our faith and our courage to walk in it that has kept us a growing and prosperous nation. We have been a nation that always clings to its faith in

God and country. Although there have been many dark moments throughout our history, the majority of us have stuck to the principals that have made us a powerful nation. It has been fathers who have written into our history the fabric that has weaved us together. It was fathers first that took the steps needed to protect our beliefs even when others tried to enforce their own on us. Fathers that fought against tyranny so that we could be free to follow the standards set by God Himself. We all know that it was fathers that stood their ground even when faced with the oppression of slavery. They even took part in a war against it! It was a war that pitted fathers against other fathers from different parts of the same land those generations before died so that others could be made free. It was also fathers who took on evil dictators in the wars that followed so that their children would not have to suffer at the hands of those who believed that other ways of life were greater than the one that we already adapted. It was a father that led a race of people to push for their rights to live at the same level as other races did. It was fathers that set our sights on the moon and got us there. Fathers have advanced our technologies and given us a better way of living. We've gone from hand-written, hand-delivered mail to mail typed on a computer that can be sent anywhere in the world in seconds. All these things that I've mentioned, and many others that I did not, have been made possible by fathers over many generations. I am by no means saying they did it alone because there is no way that they could. A father who has been too prideful can attest to his failures when he has tried to go it alone. That is if he is honest. It is by design that man is to live with the help of a mate. So moms everywhere don't worry because he can't be as good as he can be without your help. But overall dads you should understand by now that your contributions to the family are numerous and never ending. You hold the key to its success or failure. Knowing this fact, you must decide on the direction you want to go to get them to as many triumphs as you possibly can. Anything great will not come easy. You have got to do the work and there is no way to get around it. There is also great pride in getting it done after all the hard work that you have done. I suggest that you strap yourself in and go for the ride of your life. It may be ruff sometimes, but it is the price that you pay to lead the way into the future. That's okay though because your character is being strengthened in the process. The sword that is your mind is being sharpened and polished. The struggle is also necessary so that we will have obstacles to overcome and conquer. After all, progress is always made when we meet and beat those challenges that come against us. This is also where male pride is a good thing as we are motivated by it after the job is finished with a positive outcome. I am convinced that there are those who feel that they are entitled to everything under the sun. They are driven by the thought that they are owed simply because they exist. Just breathing means that they should have what they want. Wisdom has proven that can't possibly be the case. It is foolishness to adapt that line of thinking. Man was given a mandate long ago that he would have to work to achieve his goals so sitting down on your rear and expecting pennies from heaven is not a smart strategy to follow. We truly have no business thinking that is good for the family. Guys, give yourself no choice but to be great at the assignment that you may pursue and not great according to the opinions of other men. It is your duty to make your mark on this landscape that is our planet and nothing less should be acceptable to you. A very wise man once said "leave empty"! This means that before you die, you should have done everything that you were destined to do. It means that your life's tank should be empty before you make your exit from the world. Men who do not even make the attempt to do so deprive many of the deposits that he is actually commanded to leave on the earth. No one is here randomly and there is a plan for each of us. So we all have meaning and purpose. I believe that every man has the potential to get the best results for each situation that he faces. As a father, I have the ability to change the world through every life that I have the privilege to touch! I don't see any goals that are greater than doing just that. Fathers! Live on and with purpose! Your life was not your own the moment you came out of your mother's womb. We should first focus on your daily meeting with the creator (Matt. 6:33) to get your instructions and then make your moves based on completing the task that you are assigned to take care of.

Nothing else matters!

Just in case you're interested:

My boys are doing very well for themselves. Garrick III is now 24 years old, he lives in San Diego and is a chef at a five star restaurant in the downtown area claiming that there is nothing that he can't cook. We do not always communicate the way I would like to or even as often, but our relationship is a work in progress and I believe that it is going in the right direction. With time and effort we'll improve and become closer. Wesley is 19 now and thinks that the hair on his face makes him a man (just kidding). He has graduated from high school and he decided to all of our surprise, to enlist in the United States Marine Corps. He has gone through boot camp, completed his military training, and he is now preparing and training for his next assignment. It should go without saying that I am very proud of the man that he is becoming. They are both showing me that my mistakes do not have to follow them and everything can work out with a lot of patience and effort! Dads don't let circumstances prevent you from doing everything necessary to be a father to your children! We are living in a time where you are more essential than you could ever imagine!

Peace be with you!

61034789R00065

Made in the USA
Charleston, SC
10 September 2016